More Civility, Please

*Make Your Corner of the World
A Better Place*

More Civility, Please

Make Your Corner of the World
A Better Place

GLENN DROMGOOLE

On the cover: The olive branch is a traditional symbol of peace. Astronaut Neil Armstrong, the first person to walk on the moon, left a small gold replica of the olive branch on the moon as a gesture representing a wish for peace for all mankind.

© 2016 by Glenn Dromgoole
ISBN: 978-0-9973706-0-7
Book designed by Goofidity Designs
Printed in the U.S.A.

Published by TexasStarTrading.com
174 Cypress St., Abilene, Texas 79601
info.texasstar@yahoo.com
(325) 672-9696

Contents

Dear Reader   7

More Civility, Please   9

Make Your Corner of the World a Better Place   19

We Have the Power   27

Make a Difference with Your Life   29

The Power of a Penny   33

Try Giving Yourself Away   41

A Year of Gratitude   45

Who Is In Your Hall of Fame?   49

Advice to a Young Friend   55

Tall Goals for Tall People   63

Just Three Words   67

Just Four Lines   71

An Extraordinary Ordinary Man   75

Building Bridges   77

Aha!   81

Dear Reader

This little book was originally intended for graduates – high school, college, graduate school – who are just starting to find their place in the world. But certainly we all could benefit from a little more optimism, hope, kindness, decency, generosity, respect, reason, and civility in our everyday lives, our families, our workplaces, our churches, our relationships, and especially our politics.

So I hope these words of encouragement and inspiration offer some practical thoughts on how you – wherever you are in life -- can begin, or continue, to make a positive difference in your corner of the world every day.

Glenn Dromgoole
Abilene, Texas

We ourselves feel that what we are doing
is just a drop in the ocean.
But the ocean would be less
because of that missing drop.

Mother Teresa

More Civility, Please

The world needs a generous dose of civility. Each of us can make a difference by making our little corner of the world a more civilized place. And in the process, we enrich our own lives by giving them a sense of purpose and meaning.

Civility is contagious. Catch it. Live it. Spread it. At home, at work, at school, at church. In the community, in the car, in the stadium. Talk about it at the dinner table, in discussion groups, with friends and business associates.

Here are some suggestions to get you started. You can find other ideas, and quotes, on civility highlighted throughout the book.

► Reject the temptation to criticize someone else's actions without first considering his or her side of the story.

► Respect the dignity of those whose politics, theology or world view you disagree with. Try to find some common ground.

► Whenever you're inclined to state an adamant position, consider the possibility that "I could be wrong."

► Treat everyone with a little more respect.

► Set aside one hour a week to write three notes or e-mails to people who have contributed in some small way to making this a better world.

► Think a billboard thought. Express in seven words or less a message you would want to put on a billboard for everyone to see. Live that message. (The message I would like to put on a billboard is the title of this book: More Civility, Please.)

► Make peace with someone with whom you have had a disagreement.

► Make peace with yourself for not always living up to your own standards. We all suffer lapses of civility from time to time.

► Don't be mean. Don't be rude. Don't interrupt.

► Teach your children to say "please" when they want something and "thank you" when they get something. Every time.

► Practice the "please" and "thank you" rule yourself.

► Every day look for an opportunity to make a small difference for good. Do it.

► Fight road rage by being exceptionally courteous. And patient.

► Tune out TV or radio talk shows when people start interrupting or shouting at each other.

▸ Refuse to participate in negative on-line blogs.

▸ Turn off or silence your cell phone at public events or at dinners with friends and family.

▸ Go out of your way to praise exceptional service when you encounter it.

▸ Ask yourself whether your community, your home, your workplace, church or school would be better off or worse if everyone behaved the same, or contributed the same, as you do.

▸ Try to be a little more understanding of leaders at all levels. Accord them the courtesy you would want if you were in their shoes.

▸ Make your home a place of acceptance and openness.

▸ Explain to your children what it means to be civil, kind, generous, reasonable. And show them.

► Encourage others by taking an interest in what they have to say.

► Make it a point to do something extra for someone else whenever you can – without taking or expecting any credit.

► Hold your tongue when you feel the urge to make a vicious remark.

► Don't let things become too important.

► Keep your word.

► Use good manners – holding open a door, giving up your seat on a bus or subway, letting someone go ahead of you – as a way to say to other people that you respect them.

► Accept the imperfections in others, just as you hope they will accept yours.

► Look for the possibilities, not just the obstacles.

▶ Don't be a grouch. Don't be a whiner.

▶ Walk through life with a thankful spirit, and others will want to walk with you.

▶ Remind yourself that you have the power to help people. Make it a priority.

▶ Be an advocate for reason.

▶ Question any beliefs that put people down or try to keep them down.

▶ Refuse to accept the one-sided ravings of ideologues and fanatics with simplistic solutions to all the world's problems.

▶ Don't be blindly partisan. Be open to the possibility that there may be some right and some wrong on both sides.

▶ Choose to make the world a little better because you're here, rather than a little worse.

▸ Don't argue religion. Just practice it.

▸ Practice good sportsmanship. Applaud good plays by the opposing player or team.

▸ At children's sports events, show up to encourage and support them, but keep your mouth shut.

▸ Have a conversation with someone from another faith or political belief. Try to learn something rather than argue the superiority of your own view.

▸ Be known as someone who is easy to get along with.

▸ Find a quotation that you believe has something important to say about civility and include it on your business card.

▸ Teach your children that the true joy of life comes from giving, not getting.

▸ Cook something and take it to a neighbor. Sharing food makes the world a little more civilized.

► Don't put off doing the good things you think about. Act on your good intentions.

► Be the kind of cheerful person you enjoy being around.

► Support local artists, musicians, authors, poets, actors in their creative endeavors.

► Remember those who risk their lives to protect us. Send a card to your local police or fire department or military installation. Make a donation to a charity in their name.

► Hug a teacher. Thank a school board or city council member. Write a note of encouragement to an elected official.

► Bury a hatchet. Mend a fence. Call a truce.

► Approach every day with the idea that you are going to learn something new.

▶ Every time you get the chance, vote. Never take that right for granted.

▶ Try to be someone who votes for, rather than against. There's a lot to be for in our towns, cities, states and in our country.

▶ Remember: This, too, shall pass. Keep your perspective.

▶ Slow down a little and take time to be more courteous.

▶ Believe in the future. Work to make things better. Realize that you can make a difference.

▶ Say to yourself: *Wherever I am, I can do something to make my corner of the world a better place.*

Lord, make me an instrument of thy peace.
Where there is hatred, let me sow love.
Where there is injury, pardon.
Where there is doubt, faith.
Where there is despair, hope.
Where there is darkness, light.
Where there is sadness, joy.
O Divine Master, grant that I may not so much seek
to be consoled as to console;
to be understood as to understand;
to be loved as to love.
For it is in giving that we receive.
It is in pardoning that we are pardoned.
And it is in dying that we are born to eternal life.

The Prayer of St. Francis of Assisi

One is not born into the world
to do everything,
but to do something.

Henry David Thoreau

Make Your Corner of the World a Better Place

As I approached my seventieth birthday, I got to thinking about what I've learned in seventy years that I might want to impart to my children, grandchildren, or anyone else who might be interested.

I like to make lists and so I thought about doing something like Seventy Things I've Learned in Seventy Years, or Seventy Things I Like about Living to Be Seventy, or Seventy Things I Wish I Had Known Earlier in Life.

Instead, however, I decided to boil it down to one thing I have learned – the one thing I would like to pass on to posterity.

It is this:

Wherever I am, I can do something to make my corner of the world a better place.

Wherever I am, I can do something to make my corner of the world a better place.

Just seventeen words.

Let me break that down into its four phrases: Wherever I am/I can do something/to make my corner of the world/a better place.

▸ *Wherever I am*

I have lived all my life in Texas except for one sabbatical year when I had an opportunity to live and study in Michigan. Thirty of those years have been in the same town – Abilene, Texas, a city of 120,000 mostly good folks. Abilene is 150 miles west of Fort Worth, where I also lived for about fifteen years.

Anyway, that's where I live and where I have worked and written and tried to make a small difference these past three decades. It's where I am.

But the phrase "wherever I am" applies to more than just the town where one lives. "Wherever I am" has to do with family life, with the workplace, with wherever

I visit, with whom I'm in the presence of at a given moment, with whatever situation I find myself in, with the Internet, with wherever I am at any specific time. As Max Thurman stated it so simply, "My goal in every encounter is to leave the other enhanced."

Now, of course, I don't always succeed. I don't always make "wherever I am" a better place, I don't always "leave the other enhanced." But that's the ideal, that's the goal to strive for.

More Civility, Please

- - -

Pitch in.
Help out.
Lend a hand.

► *I can do something*

One of my favorite quotations is from Henry David Thoreau: "One is not born into the world to do everything, but to do something."

And that's what each of us can do. We can do something. We can have a positive influence.

It may be nothing more than a smile and a cheerful "good morning" while serving coffee, or drinking coffee, at a breakfast diner. But it's something.

It may be writing a check to help the Salvation Army

or the Red Cross with disaster relief where folks have lost their homes to fire or storm or flood.

It may be sending an encouraging note or making a phone call to someone needing to hear a word of hope. It may be delivering Meals on Wheels to an elderly person, or helping a neighbor cope with an emergency, or baking a cake for the guys at the fire department.

It may be running for city council or school board because you want to give something back to the community, not because you have an axe to grind, or voting for a bond issue that will have a positive impact on the future of the town even though it may raise your taxes.

It may be telling a council or school board member that you appreciate his or her service.

It may be serving on a board or donating time or money to a cause or volunteering a few hours at the food pantry or the hospital or the library.

We're not expected to do everything, but we can do something.

▶ *To make my corner of the world*
The phrase "my corner of the world" reinforces, I

suppose, the first phrase in the sentence, "wherever I am."

But "wherever I am" might change from time to time. Wherever I am, today, is Abilene, Texas. Wherever I am, tomorrow, might be somewhere else. But wherever it is, it is the corner of the world that I have an opportunity to influence for good.

Chances are, most of us won't live in the same location forever. But we will be somewhere, and that somewhere is our corner of the world. I may not have a lot of power to change the world -- but I do have the power to make where I am a better place.

I know people in our city who have been able to expand their corner of the world beyond the city limits of the town.

The church I attend has made an orphanage in Romania and an impoverished Indian village in Arizona part of its corner of the world because of several folks who saw the need and called our congregation's attention to it. It has welcomed African refugees who have seen their own corner of the world torn apart by genocide.

Another group in our town reaches out to the desperate people in Haiti with food, clothing, and water resources. A friend of mine sponsors an inner city basketball clinic in the Bahamas that teaches a lot more about life than how to shoot a basket.

My daughter Jennifer's corner of the world keeps changing as she and her family move to a different country every two or three years. But while they are there, she tries to get involved and make that corner a little better. Consequently, she and her husband and children have made a wide range of lasting friendships that they cherish.

And certainly we all are connected through the Internet, through blogs, through Facebook and Twitter and other on-line communities. We can have a positive influence on these sites, rather than a negative one.

Our corner of the world is not limited to wherever we are. But it's certainly the right place to start.

▶ *A better place.*

Okay, this is subject to interpretation, for sure. What do we mean by better?

Some would interpret that politically, thinking that the only way to make it better is their way. It doesn't matter how divisive they have to get, how much name-calling is involved, how vicious the campaign – whatever it takes is worth it because they know what is best.

That is not what I mean by "better." That type of hyper-charged political atmosphere – politics by intimidation, no room for compromise – has not made this country "better," in my opinion. It has virtually torn it apart. It can tear apart communities as well.

Maybe what I mean by "better" is "nicer" or "kinder" or something like that. "More civilized," perhaps.

It's not about who's right or who's wrong. It's about making our communities, our families, our work environments kinder, gentler, friendlier, supportive, reasonable, caring. And each of us has the power to do that.

Wherever I am, I can do something
to make my corner of the world a better place.

The six basic mistakes of man are:

1. The delusion that individual advancement is made by crushing others.

2. The tendency to worry about things that cannot be changed or corrected.

3. Insisting that a thing is impossible because we cannot accomplish it.

4. Refusing to set aside trivial preferences.

5. Neglecting the development and refinement of the mind and not acquiring the habit of reading and study.

6. Attempting to compel other persons to believe as we do.

Cicero

*There is no power on earth that can neutralize
the influence of a high, pure, simple, and useful life.*

Booker T. Washington

We Have the Power

We don't have control over a lot of things in our lives. But it's easy to let that be an excuse for not using all the power we do have.

We have the power to smile.

We have the power to be kind.

We have the power to be courteous and pleasant.

We have the power to praise.

We have the power to offer a compliment.

We have the power to listen.

We have the power to encourage.

We have the power to make others feel important.

We have the power to try.

We have the power to care.

We have the power to do our best.

We have the power to be truthful and honest.

We have the power to participate.

More Civility,
Please

Say "I'm sorry."
Say "I love you."

We have the power to give.

We have the power to vote.

We have the power to be optimistic.

We have the power to be happy.

We have the power to like ourselves.

We have the power to treat others with respect.

We have the power to make a difference.

We do not lack for power. We just need to recognize it and make the best use of it.

*Wherever I am, I can do something
to make my corner of the world a better place.*

It's easy to make a buck.
It's a lot tougher to make a difference.

Tom Brokaw

Make a Difference
with Your Life

Whether you are just starting out or seeking a fresh start, you have the opportunity to make this a little better world. Here are ten simple ways to make a difference with your life.

▶ Be kind.

Make the effort to do one little act of kindness a day. Encourage others. Praise them. Be polite. Offer to help.

▶ Be generous.

Discover that the joy of giving is truly the joy of living. Give compliments. Give time. Give your talent. Give money. Give your best. Give credit to others. Give thanks.

▸ **Be optimistic.**

Optimists see the opportunities and the possibilities in life, not just the problems.

Walter Heiby tells of two salesmen assigned to sell shoes in undeveloped countries. One wired back: "This is a terrible territory. No one here wears shoes." The other sent this message: "This is a wonderful territory. Everybody here needs shoes.

▸ **Be a doer.**

Look for ways to make things better. Suggest solutions. Offer ideas. Don't fall into the trap of complaining about every little thing. Be a doer, not a whiner.

▸ **Be a communicator.**

Develop the ability to communicate one on one. Listen. Smile. Be open to others' ideas. Look for ways to bring people together. Be true to your word.

More Civility, Please

- - -

Smile more.
Complain less.
Praise more.
Criticize less.

▶ Be a participant.

Take an interest in what is going on in the workplace, the community, the world. Vote. Volunteer. Contribute. Care.

▶ Be compassionate.

You have a heart. Listen to it. Be sensitive to those in need. Help when you can. Treat people in need the way you would want to be treated if you were in desperate circumstances.

▶ Be reasonable.

Few things are black and white. Look for the shades of gray. Be respectful to those with whom you disagree. Be fair.

▶ Be curious.

Don't let yourself get stuck in a rut because of your own lack of initiative. Be open to new experiences, ideas, people, places. Develop new interests. Be passionate about life. Don't be afraid of change.

▶ Be thankful.

Approach life with a thankful spirit, a grateful heart,

a joyful outlook. We have benefited from someone else's time, interest, money, encouragement, discipline. Never take these gifts for granted.

Wherever I am, I can do something
to make my corner of the world a better place.

I am only one, but I am one.
I cannot do everything,
but I can do something.
And I will not let what I cannot do
interfere with what I can do.

Edward Everett Hale

The Power of a Penny

At first I hardly recognized it. It didn't look like much. I wasn't even sure it was what I thought it was.

I was out for a walk in the neighborhood. Sometimes on these walks I find a little money. Never very much: a penny here, a nickel there. But I always stop and pick it up, then toss it in a jar I keep change in.

On this day I spotted something that looked like a penny – sort of. I stopped and picked it up and examined it.

It was a gnarled coin. It looked like it had been run over many times. The edges were jagged. I could barely make out the face of Lincoln. One old, beat-up penny.

But as I felt of that tired, worn, flattened, tromped on, almost worthless penny, it began to take on special meaning. It became a parable to me about how each person has value, about how each of us can contribute something to our communities.

Sometimes we find ourselves feeling like that old penny. Worthless. Forgotten. Discarded. Flattened. Ugly. Worn out. Yet, like the penny, we still have value. We can make a small difference wherever we are, in whatever our circumstances, that can add up to something big.

It's easy to fall into thinking that we are little more than a drop in a bucket, that we don't have a lot of power over what's going on around us. And yet, we have one vote, which we can use to the best of our ability. We have one voice, which we can use to make a positive difference in someone else's life. We have one minute, which we can use to write someone a note or listen to someone's problem or be someone's friend.

Let's say there are 100,000 people in your city. If every person – every man, woman and child – put just one penny a day into a jar and then donated it to a good cause at the end of the year, that would amount to more than $365,000!

Another example: If everyone in that same city of 100,000 passed along one compliment a day or did one kind deed a day, in a year's time that would be more than thirty-six million compliments given or kindnesses done.

A worthless penny? Not when you figure it that way.

▸ In 1952 William Fickling planted a cherry tree outside his home in Macon, Georgia. The tree was so beautiful that he began giving clippings of the tree to his neighbors. Soon the Yoshino cherry trees were blooming all over town.

Today Macon, Georgia, is known as the Cherry Blossom Capital of the World, with more than 300,000 cherry trees. Its international Cherry Blossom Festival runs for two weeks and draws crowds of a half million people. And it all started with one man and one tree.

The Power of a Penny.

▸ On Super Bowl Sunday in 1989, a young minister prayed a simple prayer at Spring Valley Presbyterian Church in Columbia, South Carolina.

"Lord," he prayed, "even as we enjoy the Super Bowl football game, help us be mindful of those who are without a bowl of soup to eat."

The church youth were inspired to ask people to donate a dollar which would go to a local program to feed the hungry. They called it SOUPER Bowl Sunday. The idea has spread across the nation and now nets millions of dollars for local hunger programs.

It started with one prayer, and one group of young people responding to the prayer.

The Power of a Penny.

▶ Grandpa Orr lived in a small town in Nebraska during the Depression. There was a chicken thief in the neighborhood, and Grandpa Orr's chickens kept disappearing. It was common knowledge who the thief was, but no one ever caught him in the act.

Finally, one day Grandpa decided that something had to be done. He asked his wife to select a fat hen and prepare

More Civility, Please
- - -
Read more.
Write more.
Pray more.
Think more.
Listen more.
Laugh more.

it for a meal. He then took the meal to the thief's home and presented it to him and his family.

Grandpa Orr lost no more chickens after that.

The Power of a Penny.

▶ Alan Gibson, co-founder of Americans for More Civility, awards a Peace Prize every year at his local high school in Georgia. The award recognizes two students for their civilizing and peacekeeping efforts, and their names are inscribed on a plaque in the library.

What if we had a Peace Prize at every high school?

The Power of a Penny.

▶ Geography students, so the story goes, had been studying the Seven Wonders of the World, and at the end of the section they were asked to vote on what they considered the Seven Wonders of the World today.

They came up with the Great Pyramids, the Taj Mahal, Grand Canyon, Panama Canal, Empire State Building, St. Peter's Basilica, and the Great Wall of China.

While gathering the votes, the teacher noted that one student, a quiet girl, hadn't turned in her paper yet.

She asked the girl if she was having trouble with her list.

"Yes, a little," the girl said. "I couldn't make up my mind because there were so many."

The teacher said, "Well, tell us what you have, and maybe we can help."

The girl hesitated, then began. "I think the Seven Wonders of the World are … to touch … to taste … to see … to hear … to run … to laugh … .and to love."

The Power of a Penny.

▶ I read about a woman in Oklahoma who was a creative tipper. She and her husband were having lunch with some friends. Their waitress that day seemed distracted, inattentive, and generally unpleasant.

The normal response would be to leave only a token tip, if any tip at all. But this woman, Margaret, quietly pulled a twenty-dollar bill out of her purse and attached a note to it with a paper clip. The note read, "Thank you for serving us today. God bless you."

A few minutes later the waitress came back to the table, wiping her eyes. She knelt beside Margaret and thanked her. She explained that from the start that day everything had gone wrong. She knew the gift was undeserved, but it had encouraged her.

The Power of a Penny. (Well, in this case, a twenty-dollar bill, but you get the point.)

Here's an exercise. Take a penny out of your pocket or drawer or change container. Make that one penny a special penny for the next week. Carry it in a pocket or put it somewhere so you can remember it, separate from other change. Let this penny be a reminder to you of the power you have to make your corner of the world a better place.

Put that one penny to work in some helpful way.

Maybe there was a teacher or coach you especially liked in school and you haven't seen him or her in a long time. Let your penny remind you to send a note and just say thanks.

You've been intending to make a donation to an organization that helps people, but you just haven't gotten around to it. Let your penny remind you to get around to it.

You see someone at an intersection holding a sign asking for help. Let your penny remind you to count your blessings and be generous with someone in need. (More than a penny!)

You've had a disagreement with someone. Let your penny remind you to bury the hatchet.

When you're so busy that you find yourself feeling hassled and frazzled, let your penny remind you to slow down a little and take time to be more thoughtful.

Maybe your penny will encourage you to cook something and give it to a neighbor. Maybe your penny will stimulate you to begin writing that family history you've been putting off. Maybe your penny will remind you to be a little more cheerful and a little less critical for the next seven days.

It's just one penny, but it's yours.

We can have the Power of a Penny if we learn to make use of the little things in our control. Over time, they can add up to something big.

Wherever I am, I can do something
to make my corner of the world a better place.

A happy life is made up of little things
in which smiles and small favors are given habitually.
A gift sent, a letter written, a call made,
a recommendation given, transportation provided,
a cake made, a book lent, a check sent –
things which are done without hesitation.

Carl Holmes

Try Giving Yourself Away

One of my favorite books is *Try Giving Yourself Away* by Robert Updegraff under the pen name of David Dunn. It was written more than sixty years ago by a businessman who made it his hobby to find little ways to brighten someone else's day, but the concept is as valid today as the day it was written.

"I took up giving-away as a hobby," he said, "because I found that it made my life more exciting and broadened my circle of friends. I became a happier person.

"Nobody ever found real and lasting happiness

in being completely selfish --- not in the whole long history of the world. It seems to be a law of life that we enrich ourselves most when we give ourselves most fully and freely."

Here are a few of the things he learned to give away:

► A phone call to an old acquaintance he hadn't talked to in several years.

► A compliment to the chef for a good meal.

► A note to an author of a magazine article or book he enjoyed.

► An idea to a business for a slogan or an advertisement, with no strings attached.

► Finding opportunities to give credit to others.

He said there are so many things we have to give: Our time, our experience, our abilities, our influence, our understanding, our tolerance, our good will, our courage, our faith, our sense of humor, our optimism, our smiles.

Giving is not just about money. Giving is about how we decide to approach life.

"This book genuinely changed how I live," an on-line reviewer wrote just a few years ago. "It gave me a different view on what it means to think about other people, and how you can give gifts and the effects it can have."

"I read it," wrote another reviewer, "then I lived it. I still do."

David Dunn, or Robert Updegraff, called giving-away "the finest heart tonic in the world" because it not only lifts one's spirit but he believed it stimulates circulation and "makes you feel alive and full of health."

More Civility, Please

· · ·

Volunteer.
Recycle.
Forgive.

As far as I know, *Try Giving Yourself Away* is out of print now. But you can find it on most used book web sites. I look for it at the used book sale that our Friends of the Library put on every summer.

I consider it a successful sale if I can find a copy of that book, and most of the time I do.

And, then, I take great pleasure in giving the book away and telling the person I am giving it to why it is my favorite book. I keep a few extra copies on my bookshelf so I can give the book to someone on an impulse.

"The secret of successfully giving yourself away,"

wrote David Dunn, "is not so much in calculated actions as in cultivating friendly, warm-hearted impulses. You have to train yourself to obey giving impulses on the instant – before they get a chance to cool. When you give impulsively, something happens inside of you that makes you glow, sometimes for hours."

I came across a quote from Fred Rogers (*The World According to Mister Rogers*) that fits in with what David Dunn/Updegraff wrote about.

"The real issue in life," Mr. Rogers said, "is not how many blessings we have, but what we do with our blessings. Some people have many blessings and hoard them. Some have few and give everything away."

Try giving yourself away. It is never too early, or too late, to start.

Wherever I am, I can do something
to make my corner of the world a better place.

God gave you a gift of 86,400 seconds today.
Have you used one to say "thank you"?

William Arthur Ward

A Year of Gratitude

How often do you write thank you notes to people who have given you a gift or just done something nice for you?

John Kralik, a lawyer in California, wrote a book a few years ago, *365 Thank Yous*, about a special year in which he went out of his way to remember to thank people. The subtitle of the book is *The Year a Simple Act of Daily Gratitude Changed My Life*. He followed up that book with another entitled *A Year of Gratitude*.

Kralik's life was at perhaps its lowest ebb as he approached the new year of 2008. His law practice was nearly broke and was losing its lease, he had gone through his savings trying to keep his business and his various mortgages solvent, he was in the middle of a second divorce, his girlfriend had broken up with him, and he was worried he might lose his seven-year-old daughter. He was frustrated, angry, tired, depressed.

But on a walk one morning, he said he heard a voice that clearly spoke to him: "Until you learn to be grateful for the things you have, you will not receive the things you want."

As he walked, he decided to embark on a year of trying to be more grateful. "I would try to find one person to thank each day. One person to whom I would write a thank-you note."

As the year progressed, his attitude changed, and so did his life. His business did better. He reconnected with friends he had neglected over the years. He became closer to his family. Despite financial setbacks from the stock market crash that fall, he ended the year better off physically, mentally, emotionally, and economically.

It would take him fifteen months, not twelve, to complete his goal of writing 365 thank-you notes, but at the end he would conclude: "Writing thank-you notes is a good thing to do and makes the world a better place. It also made me a better man. More than success or material achievement, that is what I sought."

Not only did it change his life, it also had a positive impact on the hundreds of people who were on the receiving end of his notes – his co-workers, clients, court adversaries, family, friends, the people who served him coffee or cut his hair. And then he touched thousands more by writing a book about it.

These days, if we do send thank you notes to people, it's more likely to be in the form of an e-mail than a handwritten note or card. And I think that's fine. Some older folks might prefer to get a handwritten note or card, but we're talking about format here, not substance. The important thing is not the way the message is

More Civility,
Please
- - -
Count your blessings.
Count them again.

delivered, but the spirit in which it is offered. However, if you're writing your grandmother, you probably ought to handwrite it.

A year of gratitude:

*Wherever I am, I can do something
to make my corner of the world a better place.*

It is said an Eastern monarch
once charged his wise men
to invent him a sentence to be ever in view,
and which should be true and appropriate
in all times and situations.
They presented him with the words:
"And this, too, shall pass away."
How much it expresses!
How chastening in the hour of pride!
How consoling in the depths of affliction!

Abraham Lincoln

Let us be grateful to people who make us happy.
They are the charming gardeners
who make our souls blossom.

Marcel Proust

Who Is in Your Hall of Fame?

The National Baseball Hall of Fame in Cooperstown, New York, is one of the oldest and grandest of the sports halls of honor. Today all pro sports have halls of fame, most individual colleges do, even high schools. There are local and regional and state halls in sports, music, and various other endeavors.

But what about your own personal Hall of Fame? Who would you select? Who has meant so much to you at some point in your life that you would unanimously (well, you're the only one voting, after all) elect them to your Hall of Fame?

I remember a fifth grade teacher, my first male teacher, who drilled us in math so fervently that it just became ingrained in my mental DNA. There was a kindly seventh grade teacher, another man, who would let us listen to the World Series on the radio back when the games were played in the daytime. He also was a stickler in math and made it fun.

A coach gave me a chance to play even when I wasn't very good. A man in our town treated me like one of his own family when I needed an adult friend besides my parents. A history teacher granted me a good grade on a term paper even though he completely disagreed with my political premise. An English teacher taught me a respect and reverence for poetry.

I think about college professors who encouraged and challenged me and bosses who gave me a chance and let me have some freedom to try ideas that were a little outside the box. There was a Sunday school teacher after I was grown who lived with integrity and died with dignity.

Of course, my parents would go into my Hall of Fame and my wife Carol and my children and grandchildren and my brother and several aunts who were always supportive. Good friends like Charlie and Betty and Jay and Laura and Joe and Alice make it, mainly for their friendships but also for the things they have accomplished and the examples they have set in our community.

> ## More Civility, Please
>
> - - -
>
> Make a donation to a favorite charity in honor of someone who has been a positive influence in your life.

Andy, the UPS delivery guy who was a walking, talking, living course in customer service, goes in there, several preachers, a publisher who was most encouraging, writer pal Carlton, banker buddy Jim who loves baseball and has befriended me with some autographed memorabilia, Margaret the library volunteer whose whole being speaks of service to the community, a plumber and an air-conditioning serviceman I can always count on, a mother-in-law who cooks my favorite foods, a father-in-law who was the kindest man I ever knew. The list goes on.

My Hall of Fame doesn't include many political or high-profile people, powerful leaders, well-known celebrities, or the like. They haven't had much impact on my little corner of the world, and after all this is my Hall of Fame.

However, there are some people elected to my Hall whom I don't know but have admired from a distance, and they have touched my life. Several writers come to mind, a musician or two, a few entertainers who raise my spirits, public figures whose integrity I admire.

So, what about you? Can you begin to make a list of people who have had such an influence or have been such an example that you automatically put them in your Hall of Fame? Your list will grow as you move along, but you don't have to wait to the end of your life to select people for inclusion.

Now, here's the part that I need to work on, and you probably do, too. Now that I've elected folks to my Hall of Fame, I need to let them know. What good is it to be inducted into a Hall of Fame and not know about it?

I should write a note something to the effect: "Dear So-and-So, I just wanted to let you know that I have unanimously elected you to my Personal Hall of Fame because of what you have meant to my life. There won't be a plaque, but please know that your influence is indelibly inscribed on my heart. Thank you for being there for me. Sincerely…"

Who is in your Hall of Fame? The voting begins now and continues the rest of your life.

Wherever I am, I can do something
to make my corner of the world a better place.

Civilization is a stream with banks.
The stream is sometimes filled with blood
from people killing, stealing, shouting
and doing the things historians usually record,
while on the banks, unnoticed,
people build homes, make love, raise children,
sing songs, write poetry and even whittle statues.
The story of civilization is the story
of what happened on the banks.

Will Durant

Three things in human life are important:
The first is to be kind.
The second is to be kind.
And the third is to be kind.

Henry James

Advice to a Young Friend

Some thoughts about getting the most out of life

My young friend,

Life is good. It may not always seem like it, especially during the confusing years of adolescence. But it is.

You will get more out of life if you learn a few simple truths.

Be thankful. Be helpful. Be generous. Be considerate. Be open to new ideas. Treat other people the way you would like to be treated.

To be fully human, to be happy and satisfied and successful, we eventually have to recognize that giving is ultimately more rewarding than getting. That getting along with others is ultimately more effective than being at odds with them.

So, we try to be courteous, not because it is expected or demanded of us, but because it produces the best results.

We try to be more generous, not for external reward or recognition, but for the internal satisfaction we receive from it.

We try to do what is right, not to keep from being arrested or criticized, but because everything seems to work better when people do the right things.

> More Civility, Please
>
> - - -
>
> Control your anger.
> Watch your language.
> Don't let your words
> hurt others.

We try to treat others the way we want to be treated, not because of some creed or dogma, but because in the end that makes sense.

Included here are a few practical things for you to think about, perhaps discuss with your friends, even your parents. If I sound a bit old-fashioned, I suppose that's because I am. I believe that we all have the opportunity and the power to make the world a little better place. I do. You do.

The following aren't rules, just suggestions. But my

experience is that they work, and I believe they will work for you. Life is good. Enjoy the journey.

▸ **Look people in the eye when you speak to them.** They will take you more seriously, and you will find it easier to relate to them also.

▸ **Say please and thank you without being prompted.** If you ask for something, say please. If you're given something, say thank you. Make that your rule. It will serve you well the rest of your life.

▸ **Pass out a lot of compliments.** They don't cost anything, and they will help you see the good side of life. Compliment your mom's or dad's cooking. Compliment a friend's outfit. Compliment people who do thankless jobs at school and in the community.

▸ **Write a brief thank you note when someone does something nice for you.** These days it's acceptable to send a thank you note by e-mail. But a lot of people your grandparents' age still prefer a handwritten note. The important thing is to sincerely express your appreciation in a timely manner.

▶ **Don't go around feeling sorry for yourself.** You actually have it pretty good. If you doubt that, think about those who are not as well off.

▶ **Find something every day to be thankful for.** Gratitude is one of the principal keys to a happy life.

▶ **If you get a summer or part-time job, do it enthusiastically.** Don't go into a job with a half-hearted attitude. Learn all you can from the job and from other workers. Put everything you can into it, and you will get a lot more out of it.

▶ **Turn off the cell phone.** Cell phones are wonderful, in their place. But not when you're out to dinner with family or friends. Turn off the phone. Focus on the people you are with.

▶ **Shake hands firmly.** A firm handshake communicates interest and confidence. A wimpy handshake communicates a lack of interest in the other person and a lack of confidence in yourself.

▸ **Don't do drugs, booze or tobacco as a teenager.**
Drugs and alcohol can mess up your young life big time.
Tobacco will, in fact, shorten your life, and, besides, it's a
nasty and expensive habit to pick up and an extremely
hard one to break.

▸ **Understand that you still have a lot to learn.**
Knowing that is the first step toward wisdom. You will
always have a lot to learn.

▸ **Enjoy talking with and listening to your
grandparents.** They have seen so much of life and
have experienced more changes than any generation in
history. Appreciate their company. Listen to their stories.
Learn from them.

▸ **Read more books.** Make reading a habit to be
enjoyed, not endured. Find a contemporary writer you
like and read everything he or she has written. Read
some writers you haven't read before.

▸ **Appreciate diversity, rather than expecting everyone to be the same.** We tend to hang around those who are like us, but don't limit yourself to just your group. Be friends with peers who are different, or at least be accepting and tolerant.

▸ **Donate money to a worthy cause.** Learn firsthand the joy of giving, and be generous with your resources the rest of your life. Generosity is another of the principal keys to a life of contentment and satisfaction.

▸ **Believe in yourself.** You are going to experience some rejection, disappointment, and failure. Keep your perspective. You are a person of worth and promise.

▸ **Don't let your peers determine your priorities or values.** It is not easy to stand up for what you believe, but in the end you will be stronger for doing it. Although it doesn't seem like it sometimes, in the long run others will respect you for doing what you think is right. More importantly, you will respect yourself.

▸ **Be true to your word.** If you say you're going to do something, do it. Be dependable.

▸ **Hug your parents every day.** You never know when you might not get another chance.

▸ **Find a responsible adult friend you can confide in or turn to for advice.** An objective grown-up outsider can help you see things in ways that sometimes parents cannot.

▸ **Don't let yourself get bored easily.** With all there is to see, to read, to experience, how can you be bored? Although it may seem difficult, learn to savor those moments when you are alone, even those quiet nights when you're at home instead of out on a date or running around with your friends.

▸ **Try to see things from the other person's point of view.** It isn't easy to do, but try to put yourself in his or her place and take an objective look at the situation. That doesn't mean you have to agree with or accept that perspective, but it might help you understand it.

▸ **Go out of your way to be kind and considerate -- in all situations.** "Three things in human life are important," said the writer Henry James, "The first is to be kind. The second is to be kind. The third is to be kind." The best place to start is at home.

▸ **Look up the meaning of the word "integrity."** Make it an important part of your vocabulary.

▸ **Make your corner of the world a little better place.** You have the power to do that.

Wherever I am, I can do something
to make my corner of the world a better place.

Think little goals and expect little achievements.
Think big goals and win big success.

David Joseph Schwartz

Tall Goals for Tall People

When my daughter Janet was ten, she suggested one day that we go over to the nearby elementary school and shoot baskets. She was just learning how to play basketball, and it was a beautiful day. So off we went.

The school was better than the park, she said, because the school had eight-foot goals as well as the standard ten-foot goal. A ten-year-old is not much of a match for a ten-foot goal.

But when we arrived at the school, the eight-foot court was occupied. Not by ten-year-olds, but by a group of young men who were having quite a time slam-dunking the short hoop.

My ten-year-old was disappointed. The tall people, she said, should shoot at the tall goal and let the short people use the short goal.

As it turned out, the young men were most gracious. As soon as they saw her coming, they moved over to the regulation court and left her the eight-foot basket.

But I noticed that as soon as we left, they were back over on the eight-foot court, slam-dunking and pretending they were pro basketball seven-footers.

More Civility, Please

- - -

Spread a little optimism wherever you can.

I thought about how that's the way we live life too often – shooting at the short goal, doing what comes easy rather than taking aim at a higher goal that requires more skill and effort and patience. We take the easy course, too many of us do, setting goals that are no challenge to reach.

But we are fooling no one but ourselves, just as those young men were fooling no one but themselves that they could really slam-dunk. And, in the long run, we don't even fool ourselves.

The real challenge in life comes not from the short goals that are easy to reach but from higher goals – harder goals – that require us to work, to polish our skills, to reach beyond ourselves.

Tall people, the ten-year-old said, should shoot at tall goals.

Wherever I am, I can do something
to make my corner of the world a better place.

*It's rather embarrassing
to have spent one's entire lifetime
pondering the human condition
and to come toward its close and find that
I really don't have anything more profound
to pass on by way of advice than,
"Try to be a little kinder."*

Aldous Huxley

What doth the Lord require of you?
To act justly, to love mercy,
to walk humbly with your God.

Micah 6:8

Most good advice can be expressed in
Just Three Words

Tell the truth.

Be on time.

Spend time alone.

Read more books.

Fall in love.

Find your way.

Sing out loud.

Pray for others.

Offer your support.

Cook something delicious.

Tell your stories.

Explore your past.

Be very generous.

Always be yourself.

Give your best.

Keep it simple.

Love your community.

Keep your promises.

Call your mother.

Write your story.

Expect the best.

Praise works wonders.

Laugh a lot.

Visit relatives' graves.

Climb family trees.

Support street musicians.

Always be kind.	Always be considerate.
Check the mirror.	Like your image.
Give your best.	Make it count.
See it through.	Show the way.
Take your time.	Keep hope alive.
Know your heart.	Open your heart.
Follow your heart.	Just say yes.
Just say no.	Just say maybe.
Keep looking ahead.	See the possibilities.
Focus your efforts.	Make your mark.
Embrace the future.	Take good advice.
Save your money.	Give your money.
Money isn't everything.	Stay at home.
Explore the world.	Learn from others.
Keep your friends.	Adopt a pet.
Give someone hope.	Feed the homeless.
Put others first.	Clap your hands.
Wash your hands.	Remember to flush.
Brush your teeth.	Wash your hair.
Don't smell bad.	Register to vote.
Pay your taxes.	Express your opinion.
Eat more fruit.	Eat more vegetables.
Savor good food.	Take more pictures.

Keep a scrapbook.

Set your priorities.

Open your mind.

Be at peace.

Smile more often.

Write it down.

Look it up.

Count the costs.

Enjoy the ride.

Open your eyes.

Count to three.

Think it over.

Think you can.

Keep a secret.

Spread good cheer.

Make it happen.

You're the greatest.

Collect more art.

Greet your neighbors.

Rest your soul.

Keep your cool.

Be a friend.

Play it up.

Understand the risks.

Take a chance.

Observe the scenery.

See their point.

Wait a minute.

Think it through.

Wait your turn.

Shake hands firmly.

Lighten the load.

Keep in touch.

Enjoy the day.

Wherever I am, I can do something
to make my corner of the world a better place.

Do all the good you can,
by all the means you can,
in all the ways you can,
in all the places you can,
to all the people you can,
as long as ever you can.

Attributed to John Wesley

To achieve greatness:
start where you are,
use what you have,
do what you can.

Arthur Ashe

Just Four Lines

I call these short verses "snapshot poems." In just four lines, they offer a snapshot, I hope, of something worth thinking about.

This Day
Be still
and know
that life
is gift.

First Peek
At the first peek
of daylight
I give thanks
for another day

Respite
Turn off the TV
and silence the phone
and bask in the serenity
of a quiet night alone

A New Day

Were these flowers
that colorful yesterday
or was I just not
paying attention?

A Walk in the Park

A walk in the park,
a vigorous stroll,
it's good for the heart
and great for the soul.

In the Spirit

A spiritual life, it's been shown throughout time,
doesn't require tomes of a doctrinal plan.
It's simply trying in all things to be kind,
and doing for others whatever we can.

A Religious Question

Do we want
to argue
our faith –
or practice it?

All We Ask

A grateful heart
a loving soul
a generous will
an humble spirit

Give the World a Smile
It's something anyone can do,
an adult or a child;
we all have it in our power
to give the world a smile.

Pass It On
If you've been the recipient
of a kind word or deed,
don't let it stop there –
pass it on, plant a seed.

Benediction
May your days be filled with beauty
your hours with joy
your moments with peace
and your life with grace.

*Wherever I am, I can do something
to make my corner of the world a better place.*

The fruit of the spirit is
Love
Joy
Peace
Patience
Kindness
Goodness
Faithfulness
Gentleness
Self-control.

St. Paul, Galatians 5:22-23

The work an unknown good man has done
is like a vein of water flowing hidden underground,
secretly making the ground green.

Thomas Carlyle

An Extraordinary Ordinary Man

He was, the newspaper said in its tribute to him, an ordinary man. He didn't hold office, or sit on important boards of directors, or head up a large corporation.

He just went about doing good wherever he saw a need.

If there was something that needed doing at his church, he could always be counted on to help.

If a neighbor's yard needed mowing, he took care of it.

If an elderly person needed a ride to the doctor's office, he provided it.

If someone needed an encouraging word, he was there with one.

He enjoyed life, and he enjoyed people, and people liked him.

He devoted his life to his family, his church, his friends.

More Civility, Please

- - -

Take pride in where you live.

This ordinary man wasn't that well known in his community. He was hardly known at all outside it. But to those who did know him, his gentle goodness, his loving concern for others made him, in their eyes, an extraordinary ordinary man.

Wherever I am, I can do something
to make my corner of the world a better place.

We build too many walls
and not enough bridges.

Isaac Newton

Building Bridges

I don't know if I am related to the Tennessee poet Will Allen Dromgoole, but I certainly claim a kinship. Her wonderful poem, "The Bridge Builder," has been a favorite in the Dromgoole family for as long as I can remember.

My father quoted it often. Even after he developed Alzheimer's and couldn't remember people's names, he could still quote "The Bridge Builder" flawlessly. We read the poem at his funeral.

Darrell Royal, the legendary football coach at the University of Texas, had difficulty making public speeches early in his coaching career. A friend gave him "The Bridge Builder" and told him to learn it and quote it by heart, and that helped him get over his fear of speaking.

"It tells a beautiful story," Royal said, "and I would wind up a lot of my talks with that -- about the youth and what a great commodity they were and what a great asset they were. It wasn't oil and it wasn't money that were our greatest assets. It was our young people. And we all should be trying to build a bridge for them."

The great inspirational author and minister Norman Vincent Peale included the poem in his book, My Inspirational Favorites. People have sent me copies of the poem that have appeared in anthologies, civic group newsletters, magazines, and other publications all over the world.

More Civility, Please

- - -

Always try to take the high road.

Will Allen Dromgoole (1860-1934) was the poet laureate of Tennessee and literary editor of the Nashville Banner. She also wrote several children's books. But she is best known for this poem, with its simple, eloquent, and relevant message about the quiet ways people can make a difference with their lives.

All of us have an opportunity to build more bridges.

The Bridge Builder

By Will Allen Dromgoole

An old man traveling a lone highway,
Came at the evening cold and gray
To a chasm vast and deep and wide,
Through which was flowing a sullen tide.
The old man crossed in the twilight dim,
The sullen stream held no fears for him;
But he turned when safe on the other side,
And built a bridge to span the tide.

"Old man," cried a fellow pilgrim near,
"You're wasting your time in building here.
Your journey will end with the closing day;
You never again will pass this way.
You have crossed the chasm deep and wide,
Why build you this bridge at even-tide?"

The builder lifted his old gray head;
"Good friend, in the path I have come," he said,
"There followeth after me today
A youth whose feet must pass this way.

This stream which has been as naught to me,
To that fair-haired youth may a pitfall be;
He, too, must cross in the twilight dim –
Good friend, I am building this bridge for him."

*Wherever I am, I can do something
to make my corner of the world a better place.*

Write it on your heart that every day
is the best day in the year.

Ralph Waldo Emerson

A Parting Word
Aha!

Most of our days,
most of our years,
most of our lives
are punctuated
with periods, commas,
colons, semi-colons,
and question marks.

But when we look back,
we cherish those
special moments
when the only
appropriate response
was, without question,
an exclamation point!

May your days – your years – be filled with
exclamation points as you make your corner
of the world a better place!